we are carried

sara rian

Copyright © 2022 Sara Rian
The moral right of the author has been asserted.
All rights reserved.
No part of this publication may be reproduced, stored in a retrieval system, or transmitted, in any form or by any means, without the prior permission in writing of the publisher, nor be otherwise circulated in any form of binding or cover other than that in which it is published and without a similar condition including this condition being imposed on the subsequent purchaser.

ISBN9798837874666

This book is dedicated to the ones i carry.

• • •

we are carried.
in bellies. in arms.
in love. in hope.
in caskets. in urns.
in grief. in memories.
our whole lives
and into the next
we are carried

we are carried
sara rian

grief's little garden.
talked about in quiet
whispers
by those who have
mourned.
only after you
lose someone
will you see it there.
sitting behind the old shed
or the other side of a hill.
its paths and walkways
may be paved. gravel. dirt.
you might feel confused.
what could possibly
grow from death?
the answer is
so many things.
all planted with pain.
all rooted by grief.
the bones start blooming.
what appears above ground
could be lovely. or plain.
some sweet. some bitter.
new fears crop up.
new meanings do too.
anxiety. love. anger.
gratitude.
vines. flowers. grasses.
shrubs.
it will change color.
texture. size.
but the garden will never
disappear...

we are carried
sara rian

this garden is not
a silver lining.
it is not a happy ending
or a sugarcoated reason
falling from a mouth
attempting to comfort you.
it is not the purpose
behind their death.
it is just there afterward.
a place that everyone
will stumble into
with swollen eyes.
and broken hearts.

at first you might stand still.
eventually you wander.
later you sit with intention.
to tend and learn.
to grieve and accept.
to welcome yourself
and possibly teach others.
grief's little garden
has no expectations
beyond just knowing
we all must walk in it
one day.

we are carried
sara rian

i can't believe my body has figured out how to survive
even a minute without you. let alone years.
i can't believe that my heart
remembers to beat
each day.

we are carried
sara rian

with every turn
around every corner
my heart pounces
with the hope
of seeing you.

we are carried
sara rian

i've found many things
since you left.
but that part of me.
the one that lit up with you.
that is just as forever gone
as you are.

we are carried
sara rian

the letter you wish they'd left:

you must be angry. it's only natural. what i've done changes so many things for you. i will not try to stop you from being angry. in fact, let me have it. place it in my hands as they rest on my chest. i want to take every bit of it with me. and it off of you. please do not be angry with yourself. you only have so much power. you weren't meant to have it here. let all the blame and questioning and anger fly away with me. don't let your heart be burdened with anything but getting used to emptier spaces around you. eventually, i hope the weight you feel in your chest is only me curled up in your heart. i promise i am safer there than i ever was here. i love you.

we are carried
sara rian

there will always be
a seat at my side
and space in my hand
left empty for you.
please fill them
in whatever way
you can now.

we are carried

sara rian

sometimes when i close my eyes
i see your face from that day.
the day i walked into a heavy velvet room
and i thought my heart would stop like yours.
your sweet brown eyes never opened.
and it broke us to see a frown resting
where a smile usually gleamed.
i hated seeing you like that
after knowing you died so sad.
i knew it wasn't you anymore
yet i still asked my dad
to bring you a blanket
and stay with you longer.
i forcefully blink as if
i can flush away the memory
and i drag my thoughts elsewhere.
until they eventually wander
back into that velvet room.

we are carried

sara rian

the sky offered you rest.
come with me, it said.
the earth gripped you tighter.
but you grabbed the sky's hand
and off you went one evening.
the earth is weeping still.

we are carried
sara rian

some days i am okay.
other days i find myself staring
into your old mug that i took.
hundreds of scratched circles
from years of stirring coffee.
i see the mug in your hand
along with a morning cigarette.
sleepy eyes with a bright smile.
and my okay heart
comes undone.

we are carried
sara rian

nightmares woke you
whenever you slept.
rest now, my love.
they won't bother you
anymore.

we are carried
sara rian

my love couldn't save you.
but yours saves me
over and over
again.

we are carried
sara rian

no one deserves eternal peace more than you do.
and i hope you've found it wherever you are.
i understand that you may need to shed
all that existed in your life here.
but i selfishly hope your soul
never forgets our love.

we are carried
sara rian

you left us
in the summer.
now warm air
carries an ache.

we are carried
sara rian

sometimes
i think i could cry
you back to life.

or loud enough
that you'll hear me
and come home.

we are carried
sara rian

the grief is all i have left.
i let it sink its teeth into me.

we are carried
sara rian

you may have thought
you were not needed here.
but even the sun misses your smile
and the moon prays for one more night.

we are carried
sara rian

as selfish as my grief might be
i miss the way you loved me.

we are carried
sara rian

death sat down
in a field of flowers.
picked one up and
plucked its petals.
my loved ones died.
my world crashed down.

and death picked up
another flower.

we are carried

sara rian

maybe i died with you.
and right now i'm resting
peacefully on your shoulder.
and the life that came after you
was just how a ghost dreams.
maybe we're in another universe.
i'm watching you sip coffee
and a cigarette burns in the ashtray.
maybe i just like to wonder
about any possible way
that we are still together.

we are carried

sara rian

it's been a while since
you've visited me
in a dream.
i hope that means
you've been with me
in the daylight.

we are carried
sara rian

a thousand years and a day
would still be too soon
to lose you.

we are carried
sara rian

i think of your face. your voice. your hands.
to remind myself every day that it was real.
you were here.
and you were ours.
just a quick reminder
before i crash into your death again.

we are carried
sara rian

i sit in between
the black and white.
the pain of your death
and memory of your life.
settling into this gray
we know as grief.

we are carried
sara rian

yesterday was a hard day.
and i missed you.
today was a good day.
and i missed you.
i don't know what
tomorrow will bring.
but i. will. miss. you.

we are carried
sara rian

i close my eyes
and pretend you're here.
attempting to keep you
long enough to feel whole
and short enough
that when they open
i don't mourn you
all over again.
maybe one day
it will work.

we are carried
sara rian

when we celebrate below you
holidays. weddings. births.
i hope you can only feel joy
and beg you don't feel grief.
you would never want this
but i hope those left on earth
are the only ones feeling pain
anymore.

we are carried
sara rian

some days
i drown in guilt
because i am here
happy. peaceful. alive.
and you are not.

but most days
i imagine you looking
from wherever you are
and can feel at least
two of the three.

we are carried
sara rian

your voice
has not been spoken in years
but my heart will not forget it.
it dances to the memory every day.

we are carried
sara rian

when will it sink in
that you are truly gone.
when your youngest gets married
and you're not next to me fixing her hair.
when my child takes her very first steps
and i call your disconnected number.
when i wake up on the day i turn 56
and realize i'm older than you.

it won't be any of these moments.
because the day it sinks in
that you are actually gone
will be when i'm gone too
and my hand is back in yours.

we are carried
sara rian

your love left marks in my skin
lasting longer and digging deeper
than any needle and ink could.
it will never be forgotten.

we are carried
sara rian

they need to know
that talking about you
brings you to back life.
with every spoken word
and resurfacing memory
you slowly appear near me.
and you stay as i spout love.
for a while there is closeness
between a griever and a ghost.

we are carried

sara rian

my whole life is different.
these years have changed everything.
where i live. who i'm with. what i do.
but to me, you are still sitting
in your rocking chair
and i will call you soon.
we will hang up the phone
and fall asleep smiling.
tomorrow will arrive
and i will call you soon.

we are carried
sara rian

my soul ignites
when you speak their name.
when you talk about their laughter.
to know they crossed the mind of another.
to know i am not the only one who feels
that they are missing here.

we are carried
sara rian

you may be gone
but our love is not a wound
expected to vanish beneath a bandage.
i will not heal from you.
and i do not want to.

we are carried
sara rian

we've tested it with distances
and we've tested it with time.
now that we are worlds apart
we must test it with both.
and again, without fail
this love of ours
holds strong.

we are carried
sara rian

how lucky i was to love you.
how tragic it was to lose you.

we are carried
sara rian

i am so proud of who you were
that i plan on talking about you
to many others. over many years.
more people may meet you
after death than in life.
and they will all be
so lucky.

we are carried

sara rian

you will not say
their name
too much.
or show the same
picture of them
too often.
if they were alive
you'd speak of them
without pause.
you'd share memories
new and old.
why should it be
any different
in death.

we are carried
sara rian

we come into this world
crying for our mothers.
we will leave it
just the same.

we are carried
sara rian

it's okay if they don't
understand this grief.
they will eventually.
we all understand it
eventually.

we are carried
sara rian

i don't need you to take my grief.
i just need you to hold my pain.
because the ones i mourn
live in both of those places
and there they will stay.

we are carried

sara rian

we didn't realize
they deserved poetry
written about them
long before they left.
or proudly shown photos
long before the last was taken.
so start writing love poems now.
and plaster your walls with pictures.
don't wait until the ones you love are gone
to start honoring them.

we are carried
sara rian

grievers don't need
to be reminded
that life is fragile.
walking behind loved ones
waiting to catch their fall.
checking for fevers
and asking if they're okay.
calling to make sure
they got home safely.
grievers know how fragile life is.
they are just trying to remember
that it is resilient too.

we are carried
sara rian

they deserve to be loved
long after they're gone.

we are carried
sara rian

their hearts no longer beat.
their lungs do not need air.
but wherever they are
their soul needs yours.
wherever they are
they love you.

we are carried
sara rian

listen to me.
you loved them
and they loved you.
laying them to rest
is difficult enough.
bury any doubt
in a deeper grave.

we are carried
sara rian

you are not living in the past
by cherishing someone you've lost.
they are supposed to be with you still.
they are your then. your now. your always.
i hope you tuck them safe and sound
into all the days ahead of you.

we are carried
sara rian

when it first happened
i'd write about grief
for hours. filling pages.
describing the feeling
in a hundred different ways.
pain poured from my fingers
and leaked from my heart.
years have passed and
it doesn't feel as easy.
is it possible to say
all that you needed to.
and the rest is just
living out every day
making sure each
is soaking with
their memory.

we are carried
sara rian

even when i'm not
beading words together on paper
i'm still creating with every breath i take.
i'm writing every moment with purpose
to craft a today and a tomorrow
that's prettier than any poem.

we are carried
sara rian

you could have the fullest heart
and under those same ribs
grief scrapes at the bone.

we are carried
sara rian

would you have stayed
if you'd known what was to come?
many believe the answer is yes.
but what could be a greater treasure
than finally finding peace.

we are carried
sara rian

yes, good things can happen
after losing your love.
but it will never be
a fair trade.

we are carried
sara rian

holding someone you love
while mourning someone you've lost
is one of life's most beautiful aches.

we are carried
sara rian

how can i have all of this
and none of you.
i became a wife
and you weren't at my wedding.
i'll soon become a mom
without my own.
i'm told it will be the hardest thing
i will ever do in my life.
but i already lived through
a text conversation that ended
and your reply that never came.
and every night without you after.

how does a heart peacefully love
the person in their belly,
the person who made her with me,
and the person in the clouds
knowing the three
will never meet
at the same time.

we are carried
sara rian

adding new lives in
won't replace the ones lost.
but it will give me the chance
to pass down the way they loved.
as strong as the sun.
as deep as the sea.

we are carried
sara rian

our hearts
don't suffer alone.
when she died
my belly was
hollowed out.
i was gutted.
emptied and aching.
my cries for her
echoed from its depth.
it's 6:26 a.m.
my belly feels so full.
a beautiful aching.
readying for birth.
this belly held grief.
it housed loss.
this belly holds life.
it houses potential.
some days it feels
this all at once.
i hold this belly
and i cherish both.

we are carried
sara rian

i was ready to thrive.
and prepared to grow.
i had so much love
with nowhere to go.
the seeds were planted
and ready to wake.
a beautiful hope starting
to replace constant ache.
my wounds were healing.
i felt more than just pain.
my mother smiled down
and then she sent rain.

we are carried
sara rian

a baby is born in love
with the beat of their mother's heart.
little ears pressed to their chest
like eavesdropping at a door.
a child grows older and may no longer
listen to the drum they once loved.
but they still shatter the day
the drum stops making
their favorite song.

we are carried
sara rian

becoming a parent
after losing one
feels like grief
is holding one hand
while breaking the other.
and tastes like candy
made out of sugar
and acetone.

we are carried
sara rian

the world kept spinning
and the people carried on.
but we were left with craters.
our days once filled with your voice
were hollowed out and only cries echoed.
we attempt to fill up on love and passing years
but we will always have emptiness here
in the world that keeps spinning.

we are carried
sara rian

when we think we cannot hold
another ounce of love
or new kind of grief
our origami hearts unfold
and make room for
our humanness.

we are carried

sara rian

he says how wonderful life is.
that it's actually quite perfect.
and my heart starts racing
as i run to knock on wood.
i'm right back on that front porch.
saying those exact words to her
the last time i saw her alive.
i know spoken words didn't cause
my world to collapse and crumble.
but i am not ready to take that chance.

we are carried
sara rian

tragic.
all this joy
your heart can't feel.
your eyes won't see.
then i notice the sky smile
and i know you are watching.

we are carried
sara rian

here i am.
submerged in the love
between a mother and child
and i can't help but wonder.
how cruel a world or mind can be
to make a parent leave this love behind.

we are carried
sara rian

life is full of
goodbyes that shatter hearts
and hellos that put the pieces back
together again.

we are carried
sara rian

you know you've suffered
when the closer you get
to beautiful things
the more you prepare
to watch them crumble.
i've come to tell you
to reach out anyway.
your touch does not destroy.
and holding back doesn't
keep things safe.

we are carried
sara rian

i've written this poem before.
a letter to you about life
at the end of a year.
another one without
your smile. and hands.
and that laugh.
another one with
voicemails. and photos.
and a bag of clothes
that i quickly open
to smell your perfume
before closing it again
so it can last me decades.

your grandsons are
growing up so fast.
two of your girls
will birth babies
in the first month
of the new year.
more sweet additions
to this growing life...

we are carried

sara rian

but i've come to accept
there are things
i'll never get back.
a certain giggle
because you let me
play like a kid.
a taurus attitude
you'd always forgive.
parts of my heart
impossible to return.
you hold them still.
they sit in your urn.

we are carried
sara rian

a butterfly on a highway.
a flower sprouting in cracked cement.
often reminding that some beautiful things
end up in cold dangerous places.
and not all will survive it.

we are carried
sara rian

i carried you
while she carried me.
it may not be
in the way i wish
but she has held you
nevertheless.

we are carried
sara rian

will you have my hazel eyes?
would your brown eyes glisten if you saw my belly?
will you have my dark hair or your dad's
kissed by the sun?
would your hair be dyed to match the colder season?
will your laugh roar like mine?
would you laugh if you heard her giggle?
will you grow fast and look older each day?
would you look different than you did before you died?

i can't wait to meet you.
i can't wait to see you again.

we are carried
sara rian

i truly can't believe
how life once handed me days
that i didn't know i could survive
and now it has given me more
than my heart can handle
in all the best ways.

we are carried
sara rian

july 15th

i woke up crying for you like i often do.
another dream of you just being my mom.
and me desperately trying to explain to you
that you are gone.

you were holding a baby
and kissing their cheeks.
first dream of grandma and this child.
you just stare and smile at me.
my teenager heart feels
a familiar frustration.
like the times you stayed so calm
when my taurus bull came out
and i couldn't understand your peacefulness.
my grief knows these moments aren't real
and eventually the sobs pull me from sleep.
but your smile never breaks.

you are still my peace
when i am in pieces.

we are carried
sara rian

my work has begun.
holding these generations together
by more than blood alone.
but through stories and words.
our connection is immortal.
our love is undying.

we are carried
sara rian

i never anticipated
the day i would wonder
if someone gave me the choice
to go back and she lives
or remain here and she's gone
that i wouldn't have an answer.
after the hours and days
of begging for that choice.

then i remember
the last thing she said.
you can let me go
you'll be okay...

we are carried
sara rian

like she knew one day
i would stop begging
and start being alright.
that one day
my life would be
so different
so full of love
that i'd struggle
to answer that question.

because a mom as good as her
would come face to face
with any god, power, or force
and ask that her children
have lives and loves
that they wouldn't trade
for anything.

we are carried
sara rian

your heart dances
under my hand.
her stretch and kicks roll
under the other.

this movement.
under my skin.
under yours.
is felt best
when we're still.

please world
let us stay here
a while.

we are carried
sara rian

momma,
please come visit them.
kiss their hands and cheeks
and sing them lullabies to sleep.
they're too little to look at pictures
and they can't dream about someone
they haven't met.

we are carried

sara rian

dear mom,

i did it.
i gave birth
to a beautiful baby.
she looks just like her dad.
i know you never got to meet him.
but i hope you see us together now.
it has been the most intense thing
i have ever done besides losing you.
i wish you were here to hold her. to hold me.
i have so many questions. actually i have one.
how were you so good at this?
i thought i appreciated your love entirely.
but under this sea of gratitude and awe
lies another ocean i will explore deeply.
i promise to never stop learning from you.
i love you. we love you.
for eternity. always.

we are carried
sara rian

i have fought
for so long
to stay whole.
to keep people
from breaking me.
then came you.
my sweet child.
the only thing on earth
that i would welcome
to split me in half.
shatter me into pieces.
for you i will fall apart
then come together again.
and i will be better than before.

we are carried
sara rian

so this is that in-between space
that everyone tried to describe
when their hearts bled motherhood.
full of crippling fear and wild hope.
feeling so defeated and powerful.
like i could crack down the middle
but could lift the earth if needed.
tears flow as i question everything.
smiles radiate as i sit with certainty
that i was meant to be your mom.
swaying back and forth between it all.
i'm ready to do this dance forever.

we are carried
sara rian

i will not bounce back.
this body created a body.
it made a heart. a soul. a life.
this skin stretched like a canvas
to house a masterpiece underneath.
my muscles thawed and melted.
my bones and flesh loosened.
my cradling arms cushioned.
i won't ask them to change.
i do not want to go back
to before this body
made magic.

we are carried
sara rian

spotted in milk and tears
my shirt sits on a round belly
softened and healing inside.
my hair is lifted and tangled
with knots and worried sweat.
you sit on my chest sleeping
and dream of my heartbeat.
when you see pictures one day
you'll skim past the dark circles
and the swollen soft body.
you will see your mother.
you will see beauty.
you will see love.

we are carried
sara rian

i needed darkness to see light
i needed pain to know peace.
i needed thirst to want rain.
and no matter how broken i've been
i needed me to have you.

we are carried

sara rian

before i conceived you
i prayed to every god
to not let me create you
if i could not keep you.
now that you are here
i asked them to only take you
if they can promise that i go too.
i cannot exist a second longer than you.

we are carried
sara rian

i'm bringing them into
this big scary world
asking for three things.
i beg the world to be
more kind and fair.
to show my child
beauty all around.
and to make sure
that i leave it
long before
they do.

we are carried
sara rian

if life chose to be cruel
and took you from me
be patient, my love.
for i would not be far behind.

i would claw my way
through the loosened dirt
grabbing fistful after fistful
until i reached your hands
and held them until my last breath.

i would walk into the flames
without a blink or a wince
letting my body melt into yours
until our ashes became one.

my body would follow you
into any place you rest on earth
and my soul just moments away
from whatever world you enter after.

we are carried
sara rian

i am not here to teach you
discomfort. cruelty. or pain.
the world will do enough of that.
i hope my arms are where you go
when your heart needs to rest
and your eyes need to dry.
i am here to teach you
love.

we are carried
sara rian

becoming a mother is beautiful.
but it's not the beauty that most praise.
it's the opposite of thinness and toned muscles.
far from taut bodies and refreshed eyes.
polished hair and unmarked skin.
entering motherhood means letting go.
not of yourself but of the idea that you're better
when you are smaller. firm. or smooth.
this calls on part of the bravery
needed to become a mom.
you will feel the grief
as it tears away.
but little by little
i hope you find freedom.
and i hope you feel loved.
by those around you
and most importantly
by yourself.

we are carried
sara rian

sweet baby girl,
your cries can be piercing.
but how i love watching
you find your voice
and hearing you
demand love.
as you grow
people will try
to quiet you
and wear you down
until you ask for less.
demand more.
don't settle.
you deserve
all of it.

we are carried
sara rian

my heart weeps as it remembers
that i cannot stay here forever.
but please know i am within you.
one day when you miss my voice
sing our song and you'll hear me.
if you reach out for me and cry
when only emptiness reaches back
just touch the pulse beneath your skin.
i am dancing through your veins.
my body may leave you, my love.
but my soul never will.
i will live as long
as you do.

we are carried
sara rian

my little hurricane.
i hope you take up space.
stretch and sprawl.
i hope your voice
can shatter stone.
when you set your sights
i hope they can pierce
through metal and bone.
if someone makes you feel
difficult to love. inconvenient.
or wants to keep you small
i hope you push forward
and let them drown
in your wake.
i hope you look fear
in the face and grin...

we are carried
sara rian

but when you do feel scared
i hope you remember
it's okay to cry rivers
and let the weight
pour from your chest.
i hope you remember
to be soft.
to fall apart sometimes.
i hope you remember
to let other hurricanes
join your winds.
but most of all
i hope you remember
if you just reach out
my hand will find yours
in any storm.

we are carried
sara rian

tiny hands reach
to a little mouth
that has never had to beg.
a fluttering little heart
that's never been broken.
i wish i could keep it like this.
those bright eyes that
have only seen kindness
will see bad one day.
i can't stop any of it.
but i will be there
when those hands
need mine.

and i will fight to make sure
they can still reach for me.

we are carried
sara rian

you are a mother.
if they left before the earth
made it around the sun.
you are a mother
if the only breath they took
was on your chest.
you are a mother
if they stayed a belly blossom
and only knew comfort.
you are a mother.
you are their mother.
you are their everything.

we are carried
sara rian

every mother
who has lost a child
is living that nightmare.
the one you tell her
that you can't imagine living.
she is beyond imagining.
she is surviving it.
stop telling her she is strong.
hold out your arms
and let her collapse.

we are carried
sara rian

father of my child
and love of my every life.
you watched my belly swell
and held my hand as i cracked open.
now your gaze rests above our baby's smile.
and seeing you there is my every wish granted.

we are carried
sara rian

he was not afraid
of this stained heart.
he calmly settled
next to the gravestone
covered in moss
pulled down his sleeve
and wiped it clean.
the debris fell quickly
and so did i.

we are carried
sara rian

if you choose to build
a life with someone
let them do the work
equally at your side.
we are too comfortable
feeling resentment
in spaces where
gratitude could be.

we are carried
sara rian

it's when you fearlessly
reach out your hand
towards me.
without even looking
in my direction.
knowing that
i'll see it
in the corner
of my eye
and my hand
will meet yours.
every time.

i love how secure
your heart is
with me.

we are carried
sara rian

i wrote about fearing forever
and then you came along
and handed it to me
wrapped in lace.
imagining forever felt better
knowing you were in it.
later, that forever
once wrapped in lace
cracked open
revealing a precious gem.
it sparkled just like you.
you gifted me another person
to cherish for eternity.
now i can't imagine
a better forever
than the one
with you and her.

we are carried
sara rian

my mother's mother drove away
from her little girls one day
and she never came back.
my mother left us too soon
after decades of being in pain.
so please let it end here.
let my daughter witness
her mother grow old.
let her pet my silver hair
and kiss my hands goodbye
after they wrinkle from life.
our blood carries heartache
into every generation.
please just let this mother
leave her daughter
without tragedy.

we are carried
sara rian

little one,

when my arms feel weak
or my mind has doubts
i remember how it felt
to be held by my mother.
how i'd give anything to feel
her warmth for another second.
and that makes me want
to hold you for the next
million years.

we are carried
sara rian

when those baby eyes
gaze intently into mine
i think they see my soul.
when they light up
and dance around the room
i think they are seeing yours.

we are carried
sara rian

the little body
i carry in my arms
will grow bigger.
the body that
once carried me
is now ash.
a reminder
that most things
change and fade.
but our love is
not one of them.

we are carried
sara rian

i hope you look at me
like i looked at her.
with love and forever
in your eyes.

we are carried
sara rian

i write so many letters.
some written for later.
and some written too late.
little words inked in love.
collecting dust and tears.

i write to a universe
too big to answer.
to my sweet child
too young to read.
to my late mother
too far to see.

some unread now.
and others forever.
but every letter
is worth writing.
as they are worth
writing to.

we are carried
sara rian

i will love you for eternity.
i will carry you always.

we are carried
sara rian

thank you for carrying these words ♥

Made in the USA
Las Vegas, NV
06 July 2024